You Had To Be There -
And I Was!

From Elvis to The Stones to The Grass Roots

by Terry Furlong

You Had To Be There — And I Was!
From Elvis to The Stones to The Grass Roots
First Edition Copyright © 2011 by Terry Furlong
Second Edition Copyright © 2025 by Terry Furlong
ISBN: 979-8-9991052-0-2

About The Author

Terry Furlong is an energetic participant in the music scene. His musical act is enjoyed today in a variety of popular personal appearances where his infectious, easygoing, crowd-pleasing manner delights audiences of all kinds.

Terry has enjoyed success in several different capacities, including guitarist, singer, published songwriter, producer and, now, author.

As lead guitarist for The Grass Roots, Terry has performed on the *Ed Sullivan Show, The Andy Williams Show* and made several appearances on Dick Clark's *American Bandstand.* He received a gold record for his outstanding guitar work on The Grass Roots' top ten hit "Temptation Eyes" and was a key contributor to the success of other hits by the group, including "Sooner or Later," "Two Divided by Love," and their top-selling album *More Golden Grass*, which also went gold.

Terry's memorable songwriting style embellishes works by a virtual who's who of major recording artists. His deeply moving "My Impersonal Life," helped catapult Three Dog Night's *Harmony* album to gold status and Terry's songs have appeared on albums by Tom Jones, John Hammond Jr., Larry Carlton, and many others.

In the recording studio and on the stage, Terry has worked and appeared with artists as diverse as Michael McDonald, Delaney & Bonnie, Smokey Robinson, the rock band Redbone, and many, many others.

Terry's own album, released on the Epic label as *Blue Rose*, garnered considerable attention and acclaim. It is still considered a classic today.

Other publications by Terry

Terry has penned a personal musical journey, *Gifts*. This easy read comes with a CD of the music described in the book. To order *Gifts* and its accompanying CD, or to view other music CDs from Terry's catalog, visit www. terry-furlong.com.

Dedication

To every musician, singer, writer and technician I have ever worked with, I thank you. What a joy to have shared the gift of music with all of you.

To my mother: I've been singing with my mom since the womb, and we sang together at her ninetieth birthday party. It doesn't get any better than that. I can't imagine my life without music. I thank God daily for that. I dedicate this book to my son Brandon, and, of course, to my beautiful grandchildren, Ava Grace, and Kloe Kay. Special thanks to Chuck Roberts, my good friend of many years. My sincere gratitude to my web guy and good friend, Mike Luther. And to Rick Cucuzza for the front cover photo.

And, here's to you, cousin Patrick Furlong, you made the whole project *so* much better.

Table of Contents

Introduction

The reason for this book is really very simple. After telling a number of these stories from the stage and at parties, it was suggested that I write them down in a book form so that maybe others could enjoy them. These stories are as true as I can remember them. It's said that if you tell the same lie enough times even you think it's true. Anyhow, these tales are told about as honestly as I can recall them. Remember, some of these stories took place in the fifties and sixties.

So, sit back and enjoy the journey — I sure did!

Terry Furlong

Chapter One:
The First Time I Met Elvis

In 1956, I was fourteen at the time, my friend Bob Luster and I went to see a movie on Hollywood Boulevard at the Fox Theatre, east of the famed Hollywood and Vine intersection. We were standing in line when Bob said, "Look who's standing behind you." So, I turned around and there behind me was this very odd character with very greasy long hair and very different style of dress.

He was wearing pants that were called "Peggers." They were kind of baggy and tight at the cuffs, white with a very thin black belt, and a pastel pink shirt with black stitching, and wearing black and white loafers. He was extremely different to look at considering the dress of the day was Levi's blue jeans with thin turned up French cuffs, no belt with belt loops removed and waistband folded over, stitching removed from the back

3

pockets and riding a little low, white T-shirts with turned up cuffs and the shoes of the day were "wedgies." Also, flat-top haircuts, very short on top, long on the sides and the back turning into a D. A. (ducktail is what they were called), and a pack of Lucky's (Lucky Strike cigarettes) were sometimes rolled up in the sleeves. This guy didn't look anything like that.

So, Bob says, "Don't you know who that is?"

I said, "No!"

He said, "That's Elvis Presley."

I asked, "Who?"

He said "Elvis Presley."

I said, "Never heard of him."

Bob said, "He's a famous Rock n' Roll star."

I said "Really? He sure is weird looking!"

Elvis was standing in line with a guy we later found out was his cousin. His cousin looked perfectly normal. He wore glasses, as I remember. Elvis was well mannered and gracious. Bob asked him for his autograph and he consented. So, we got a popcorn box in the lobby and tore it in half and he signed it to me and to Bob. I had that half of a box for a long time. I wish I had it now.

After the movie, Bob and I headed home but we stopped at Wallichs Music City at Sunset and Vine in

Hollywood. At this time it was probably the most famous record store in the world. It had music booths that faced Sunset Boulevard, and you could play the latest 45s (records) for free. It was usually packed with teenagers looking to see and be seen. A very innocent time. It was the fifties. As we parked our bicycles in front of the store, I was amazed to see a huge poster of Elvis' first album in the window. He was striking the now famous pose of Elvis in action. Wow! And I just got his autograph! Who could know that he was about to become the most famous entertainer the world would ever know? This was the first time I met Elvis.

Elvis – 1956

Chapter Two:
The Beatles Press Conference

In November 1963, my cousin Patrick Furlong moved to the USA from England and when he got off the plane he was carrying a guitar. I was already playing the guitar myself so I was delighted to see my cousin. We are about the same age, I'm six months older, carrying the guitar. It didn't take long before we were playing for hours on end, trading songs and guitar licks and planning our road to stardom. We quickly talked my younger brother, Kevin, into playing the drums and a good friend, Jeff Hittelman, into playing the bass, and The Furlongs band was born. We cut our first and only record as a band the next year.

This was before anyone in this country even knew who the Beatles were. Cousin Pat did because he was from England. This was before the Beatles' appearance on the *Ed Sullivan Show*. After that they were the biggest act in the world, and we were big fans, too.

Before long we had hooked up with a music producer named Bob Field. He had great success with a recording group made up of studio musicians that called themselves The Marketts and they had a big hit with an instrumental, "Out Of Limits." Bob had a recording studio in Hollywood, and we were exactly what he was looking for. A self-contained group that wrote our own songs and played our own instruments and sang harmony. A very commercial commodity.

One day Bob and a friend of his, Dave Hull, a local DJ from KRLA in LA, came to the studio. Dave was well-known as a good friend of the Beatles', and he was doing promotions for the upcoming Beatles at the Hollywood Bowl concert. Cousin Pat was recruited, because of his English accent and the odd ability to speak with that strange Liverpool dialect, to do voiceovers promoting the arrival of the Beatles show at the Hollywood Bowl. Dave Hull and his friend Bob Eubanks were having a press conference with the Beatles before the show at the Cinnamon Cinder in North Hollywood and, having something of an inside track, we found out about it. A chance to see the "Fab Four" in person was a very big deal in 1964.

I remember we were in the driveway at the Cinnamon Cinder with a lot of other people who had heard about this secret press conference when the limousine pulled in and, just like in the movie *Hard Day's Night*, the Beatles got out waving and greeting the crowd. We were in the throes of Beatlemania, and it was great fun.

After that we went to the Hollywood Hills above the Hollywood Bowl, and we heard the concert above the screams of the girls. You had to be there, and we were!

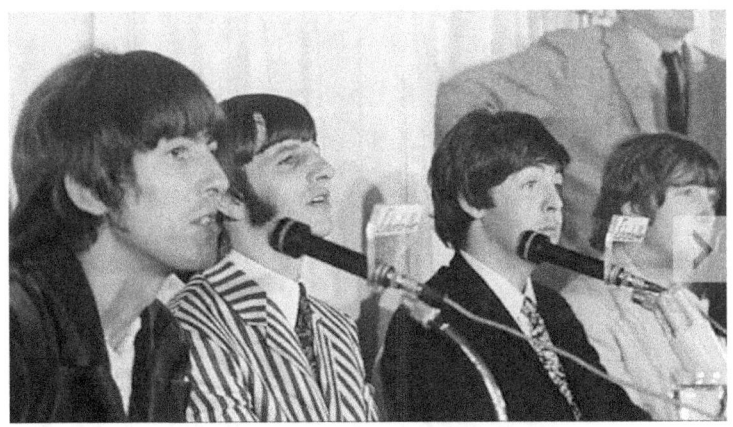

The Beatles press conference 1964

Chapter Three:
Brian Wilson Of The Beach Boys

I think the first time I met Brian Wilson was at Gold Star Recording Studios in Hollywood, California. I was working with a bass player friend of mine Harvey Sharp, who had done some work with Phil Spector, and so I wound up getting into a session that Phil was producing. Also sitting in the hall listening to Phil's session was Brian and Sonny Bono, of Sonny & Cher. We were all listening to the recording session through the door. Phil had the studio jammed with the best musicians in town.

They included two drummers, two bass players, three or four guitar players, piano players, organists, and many friends playing different kinds of percussion instruments. This was the foundation for the "Wall of Sound" that Phil was famous for creating.

The next time I remember seeing Brian was at a drive-in restaurant on Sunset Boulevard in Hollywood. He was with Marilyn Rovell, who was to become his wife and mother of his two children Wendy and Carnie. He was driving and had a carload of friends in his new 1963 Pontiac Grand Prix. The reason I remember this incident so well is because when I walked over to the car to say hi (I knew Marilyn and her sister, Diane, from Fairfax High School), he rudely rolled up the power window in my face. I don't know why he did that. I certainly didn't give him any reason that I know of. Maybe he was the possessive jealous type. I never brought it up in any of our future meetings and neither did he.

We also had a mutual friend named Arnie Geller. Arnie worked for Brian and was a very good friend of mine. One night Arnie invited Elaine Geller, no relative,

Brian Wilson (3rd from left) at Arnie's wedding

12

and me over to his house to hear a test pressing of a new record that Brian was working on. Arnie had a state-of-the-art sound system, and we were invited to his house to listen to it. He told us that what we were about to hear would blow our minds. That was an understatement!

What we heard was a record that would forever change the way recorded music was made. This was fall of 1966. The song was "Good Vibrations." The test pressing was a first generation recording, and it was absolutely incredible. The record featured cellos and the Theremin, an instrument that was predominately used in science fiction movies of the fifties to get that eerie sound. For those of you who may not be familiar with this recording, listening to it for the first time – especially with headphones – was nothing less than fantastic. Remember, this was 1966 and was probably recorded on a four-track tape recorder. Today we have ways to record that have no limit as to how many tracks we can create. I have heard that it took Brian a year to write and complete this record. The cost in 1966 dollars was staggering. His genius is a gift to us all.

The next time I saw Brian was in 1973. I had been recording some new material, and I was starting to use an ARP synthesizer that I bought from a friend named Clark Russell. Sadly, Clark died in a plane crash with Ricky Nelson while working as Ricky's sound man. I was really interested in the synthesizer after listening to Stevie Wonder's *Music of My Mind* and *Talking Book* albums, so I hooked up with his producers, Robert Margouleff and Malcolm Cecil, and asked them to work on some songs I was recording. At this time my brother, Shaun, really became interested in the synthesizer and was becoming a very good programmer. He eventually went on to program for Harry Nilsson, Seals & Crofts, Little Feat, Billy Joel, and many more.

Back to Brian.

My brother Shaun and I were together in my apartment one afternoon, when I received a phone call from Brian Wilson. He had heard about the work we were doing with the synthesizer and asked if we could come over and bring it to show to him. I told him I had the keys to the recording studio and asked him if he would like to meet us there. He said he wanted us to come to his house in Bel Air and show it to him. We went to the studio and packed up the ARP 2600 and went to his house.

In those days Brian was having a very difficult time. His problems with drugs and severe mental difficulties are well documented. When we arrived at his home he was in his bathrobe with no shirt on and was very disheveled looking. We gave him a demonstration of what the synthesizer could do and he was delighted. This,

14

coming from a man who was the master of specialty sounds on pop records, the Theremin, cellos, whistles, bass harmonicas, and the like. He then asked me to play one of my songs that he had heard about called "Let Me be the Hero of My Life." I remember playing it for him on his upright piano. Let me repeat that – I played one of my songs for Brian Wilson on his upright piano in his house. His reaction to that song was intense. He stood against the wall in the kitchen and tapped his head against the wall and stated how "heavy it was." He then proceeded to the living room and began to play snippets of Beach Boys' songs on the grand piano. *Let me say that again:* Brian Wilson played a private performance of his songs for me and my brother in his home in Bel Air. WOW! You had to be there, and I was!

Brian Wilson – in his element – the studio

15

I ran into Brian several times after that. He had hooked up with his therapist Dr. Eugene Landy and was making progress in his recovery. This was in the early eighties when they shared an office in Westwood.

The next time I heard about Brian he was on a talk show and was being interviewed about his career. This was 1995. He was talking about some of his favorite recordings and he was talking about Danny Hutton and Three Dog Night. Danny and Brian were really good friends, and he mentioned their new CD, *Celebrate – The Three Dog Night Story*, a collection of their favorites. When asked which was his favorite song, he said, "Be Still and Know." This was my song recorded by Three Dog Night on their *Harmony* album. Its real title is "My Impersonal Life." I'll bet he doesn't realize to this day that it was my song. I still have a copy of the tape of that interview. Amazing!

Chapter Four:
The Rolling Stones Session

In 1968, I was in a band called Blue Rose and we were opening for Delaney & Bonnie And Friends at a club called the Brass Ring in the San Fernando Valley. How we got the job in the first place is a story in itself. Delaney & Bonnie were supposed to play for the entire evening, four hours, but, in fact, they had only one show rehearsed and it was only an hour long.

So, it started with a casual conversation between me and my good friend Jim Price, trumpet player in Delaney's band. Jim also was in the Mad Dogs & Englishmen band with Joe Cocker and Leon Russell. Jim, of course, was the producer of "You Are So Beautiful" for Joe Cocker. Jim spent many years in the horn section for The Rolling Stones along with Bobby Keys. Jim happened to mention that they, Delaney & Bonnie, only had one set rehearsed.

I immediately sensed an opportunity and went to see the owner of the club to offer our services for the gig. He did not know that they were unprepared to play for four hours, and he gave us the gig opening for them. This was a huge break for us, because Delaney & Bonnie had been opening for Blind Faith in Europe. On top of that, Eric Clapton had joined them for an album after the tour, and they had new management and a promise of a very big promotional effort. I might also mention the lineup of musicians in this band of Delaney's because they were to become Derek and the Dominoes with Eric Clapton. They were Bobby Whitlock, Carl Radle, and Jim Gordon, co-writer, with Eric, of the iconic "Layla." More about Jim Gordon in another story in this collection.

While we were playing this gig, we were fortunate enough to meet and hang out with so many very big people in the music business. Among them were Ringo Starr, The Rolling Stones, Joe Cocker and The Grease Band, Leon Russell, The Everly Brothers, Rita Coolidge, Dave Mason, and many others.

At the end of one of these performances, Delaney asked me if I would like to go with him and Bonnie to the Stones recording session where Bonnie was scheduled to perform a vocal with Mick Jagger. I was delighted to go and we went to Electra Studios the next afternoon. The recording session was not what I expected from the

Stones. Their reputations as the bad boys of rock had me expecting a wild party. It was not. When they were working in the studio they were working. Mick was busy writing lyrics and the others were waiting their turn to contribute to the recording process.

At about this time it was suggested that we record some street noise to be added to the beginning of the album. So Charlie Watts and I went into the street on La Cienega Boulevard to make sure the microphone didn't get run into or stolen. This effect can be heard on the beginning of the album.

Jagger and Keith Richards in the studio – 1960s

The sound of the horn is what I remember coming from a white Lincoln Continental.

The whole reason for us going to the session was for Bonnie to sing a duet with Mick, and for her to do a verse by herself. The song was "Gimme Shelter." The session proceeded with Bonnie singing with Mick, and on the first take Bonnie was right on it, but Mick was not yet warmed up. The next take was better for Mick, but Bonnie was a little hoarse. Remember, she was singing every night at the club, and this was much earlier in the day. On the next take she lost her voice completely. This was to be a really big break for her and the disappointment was overwhelming to say the least. She broke down crying. Bonnie went on to have success with Delaney on several hit records, and many of you may remember her from the television show *Roseanne,* where she played Billie Joe, the owner of the diner. I always liked Bonnie, and she was always very nice to me. She even gave me some tips on my breathing technique, which helped my singing a great deal.

The session proceeded with Mick and Keith working on some vocals.

Later that afternoon a session fiddle player named Byron Berline was brought in to play on a version of "Honky Tonk Woman" called "Country Honk." In those days we all had very long hair, but Byron had a flat top haircut, and he wore cowboy boots and an embroidered leather belt with his name on it. He looked very different from all of us, and Mick and Keith thought he looked hilarious. So much so that they could not keep from breaking up. The session came to a halt. In order to continue it was decided that Byron should play out in the garden. The microphone and headphones were set up by the fountain, and the Stones could watch through a porthole in the door. They just laughed and laughed, and Byron had no idea what was going on. He probably still doesn't know. All in all, quite a fun day with the Stones.

Chapter Five:
Joe Cocker

My band, Blue Rose, was playing at the Brass Ring nightclub in Sherman Oaks, California, opening for Delaney & Bonnie when one night Dave Thomson, the bass player in Blue Rose, said while we were tuning up, "Don't turn around!" So, naturally, I immediately turned around and there sitting in the first row was a bunch of guys with very long hair that at first glance I did not recognize. Dave said "That's Joe Cocker and the *Grease Band*!" It was. Joe and the band were touring and were there to see Delaney & Bonnie. We were of course intimidated and very nervous but we played a good set.

At the end of the night, Delaney said that they were going to Leon's home studio, Leon Russell, piano-playing, song-writing legend, that is. He was a good friend of Delaney's and he was there hanging out with

23

Delaney's band that night. Leon asked if I wanted to come along. We wound up at his studio after the gig and Leon asked me if I wanted to sing on a gospel album he was doing. I was delighted and scared. Before we started I saw Joe Cocker sitting on the floor between a couple of recording machines, obviously very high. On the recording console I noticed a small piece of a joint and I picked it up and smoked it before I realized the chemical taste. Big mistake! It was PCP. From then on everything was in slow motion. But I got to be in the chorus of something we recorded. I don't know what it was but the people I sang with on that background session were amazing. It was Delaney, Bonnie, and Rita Coolidge, who went on to have her own hits, Bobby Whitlock,

Joe Cocker

keyboardist with Derek and the Dominoes, Joe Cocker and me. Wow! You had to be there, and I was!

I will always be grateful to Delaney for taking a liking to me. He's gone now but his influence on me and my generation and on people like Eric Clapton, whose first solo album was produced by Delaney, including the hit, "After Midnight," was enormous. He also produced the Dave Mason hit "Only You Know And I Know." Dave also wrote "Feeling Alright," which was a big hit for Joe Cocker in 1969.

Chapter Six:
The Grass Roots

The guys in the The Grass Roots, when I started performing with them, were Rob Grill, Warren Entner, and Ricky Coonce. Creed Bratton had already left the band and they were looking for a replacement guitarist. At the time, I was playing in a band called Blue Rose, which I had started with some friends. Warren and Rob came to see me play at this time in a club in the San Fernando Valley. I knew Warren from Bancroft Junior High School in Hollywood, and all the guys in the Roots had their hair cut by the former bass player in my first band, Jeff Hittelman. He also was my brother-in-law.

The Roots guys liked my playing and they also liked Dennis Provisor, the keyboard player and singer in my band. They asked me to join and I told them I was committed to Blue Rose and that we had a lot of irons in the fire. They asked Dennis to join the band and he accepted. They decided to try keyboards in the band and for Warren to do the guitar parts. Blue Rose continued on and I was asked to do the guitar work in the studio for the Roots.

After making several failed attempts at getting a record deal, Blue Rose was put on hold. Meanwhile I was still recording with the Roots, and one day at a session at Western United Studios I was standing by the soda machine when Warren asked me again if I would like to join the band and go on tour with them. This time, I said yes and we were to start rehearsals right away to get ready for our next dates. I had done some touring at that time but not at the level we were doing with the Roots. This was a first class operation, and we traveled all over the country in airplanes big and small, depending on where we were going and where we were playing. It was not like it is today, and the sound systems we had to use were usually underpowered and hearing what we were doing was next to impossible. So we performed the hits and did the best we could with what we had. I was disappointed but we went on with the show trying to do the best we could and not taking it all too seriously. When you can't hear yourself you just try to have a good time, and as long as we played the hits the audience was delighted. The showmanship of the group got better and better. The music did not. No one's fault. We just couldn't hear each other. What you've heard about rock bands touring on the road is mostly true, and if it sounds like I regret the experience nothing could be further from the truth. It was the experience of a lifetime.

Flying all over the country, being driven around in limousines, staying in fine hotels (well, not always), and people treating you as if you were royalty is anybody's dream. The fact that I got to do this is not something I take for granted, but at the time it was just happening and I realize now just how amazing it was. When I was growing up (like I ever did), we watched all the dance and music shows of the day, including the local shows and the national ones. The biggest of these at the time were *American Bandstand* starring Dick Clark, and *The Ed Sullivan Show*. There were others but these were the biggest. Never in my wildest dreams did I ever think that I would be on these shows.

We did *American Bandstand* several times, as I remember, and the thing that stands out in my mind is how well prepared Dick Clark was. He knew everybody by their first names, and he talked to us like we were his old friends. He made us feel right at home and we played our newest release, usually pre-recorded tracks that we sang live to. Truly great fun!

We were also guests on other very big shows, including *The Andy Williams Show* and *The David Frost Show*. We also did many other shows that were local to the area where we were playing to promote the concerts in which we were performing.

But the biggest of them all has to be *The Ed Sullivan Show*. When we did the show we stayed at the Plaza Hotel in New York City. That was the city where the show was taped. I mention this because at one time my Dad was a barber in the Plaza when I was growing up in New York some sixteen years earlier. I made a point of going down to the barber shop when we were there to say "Hi" from Tommy Furlong (my Dad) and to let them know that I

The Grass Roots on Ed Sullivan Show – me on the left

was now a guest in the hotel and was in town to tape *The Ed Sullivan Show*. My Dad was proud that I did that.

When we taped the show we had to wait in the most famous room in the history of show business, "The Green Room." When I was in that room I remember being so humbled at the thought of the stars that had been in that room. Can you Imagine? Elvis, The Beatles, Frank Sinatra, and every big star that performed there, was in that room. There were actually two rooms as I recall. They were not fancy. They were painted in a light lime green. Everything was painted – the walls, the doors, the radiator, everything. I remember looking out of the window and having that moment of "WOW, this is amazing!" I have a VHS tape of that show and I will always treasure it. I saw Elvis and The Beatles on that show, and I was on it too. I was in a rock band that performed on *The Ed Sullivan Show*. The biggest show in the history of television and show business. I consider myself honored to have done that.

When we got back to L.A. after that show I was faced with a decision that had to be made. While we were touring, I was recording some of my own songs and was working toward getting my own record deal. I decided to devote more time to this project because it was not only a dream of mine but the songs were coming out really well and I was excited about finishing them. The

Grass Roots was obviously a good thing and was about to become even better because we were having more hits. I opted for my own album and I told Warren about my decision. He was not happy about it because it meant they would have to break in a new guy and rehearse for weeks. It was not an easy decision but I had to do it. I have no regrets. I am a musician and a songwriter and the opportunity to do my own album was very appealing to me.

I had seen Rob Grill from time to time and played with him when he came to Eugene, Oregon, where I was living at the time, in 1996. We got on well and it was great fun reminiscing and playing the songs from so long ago. I received an email in 2011 from a friend telling me that Rob was in the hospital in serious condition. He had health issues for quite some time and had many operations over the years but I hoped he would bounce back again.

He did not.

I was out walking one day in July 2011, when a woman I know came up to me and said, "I'm so sorry to hear of the passing of the singer in your old band." She had heard the announcement of Rob's passing on the radio but I had not yet heard the news. A couple of days later I called The Roots drummer Ricky Coonce to talk about Rob's passing. His wife answered and when I asked to talk to Ricky she told me Ricky had a massive heart attack and died in February of 2011. I did not know. The group had not stayed in touch that much and I didn't know a thing about it. Now I find out in two days two of the guys from the band are dead. I was truly shocked and I will miss them both. Brothers in the band.

Rob Grill (left) and me

Chapter Seven:
Adventures In Touring

It has been well documented that touring in a rock band can be as exciting as life can be for a young man ready to see the world. When I was growing up we saw The Beatles in their movie, *Hard Day's Night,* and on TV on

The Ed Sullivan Show and, to quote John Lennon after he saw Elvis, "That looks like a good job." ·So, the wish of many in my generation was to be in a group that was having hit records and touring and appearing on TV. Not everyone got to do that – I did!

Me in 1965

In 1965, I received a phone call from The Sinners, a band I knew from the sixties and from hanging around Gazzarri's, a well-known nightclub on the legendary Sunset Strip. They had received a call from Jerry Naylor, the former lead singer of The Crickets after Buddy Holly died, asking me to back him at Les Poupees, a nightclub in San Jose, California, since they needed a guitar player to fill in. I was happy to do it and so my first road trip was on. It was on this trip that I met Glen Campbell.

Glen in the studio 1965

He was a friend of Jerry's and he came down to the club and sat in. He was out promoting "Universal Soldier," a Buffy Sainte-Marie song that he had recorded, and he was in the area, so he came by to visit. Glen is a fine guitar player and it was a treat to have him play with us.

My next road trip was with the band, Peter and the Wolves. I had put my name on a bulletin board somewhere and, as a result, I received a call from a guitar player, Peter Lewis, asking me to come over and play guitar with him. Peter was the son of the famous actress, Loretta Young. After playing around some, we decided to put a group together. Peter knew a drummer, Bob Newkirk, and another guitar player, Tony Bellamy, who would play bass. Thus was born Peter and the Wolves. After rehearsing, we were offered a road trip up near San Francisco, so off we went. After we finished that tour we started playing at Gazzarri's on the Sunset Strip.

Bass player, Tony Bellamy, later moved on to join Redbone with Pat & Lolly Vegas. They went on to have hits and were quite the attraction because they played in Native American dress and danced like Native Americans. And they played great! Peter Lewis went on to form Moby Grape, and had his own success.

In 1968, I left Los Angeles and moved to San Diego where I worked with a creative original band, Mother Goose. It was while playing with Mother Goose on the Sunset Strip one night that I was called to the phone by the club doorman. It seems the doorman had a guy on the

phone who wanted to talk to me. The caller, a man named Dennis Provisor, had heard me playing and wanted to know if I wanted to work a gig with him backing Dobie Gray.

Dobie had a hit record, "The In Crowd," at the

Dobie Gray 1968

37

time and had a gig playing at PJ's, a nightclub in West Hollywood. I told him I didn't know the material, and he told me not to worry, saying, "I'll walk you through it." So, that was how I met Dennis Provisor. We spent the next ten years playing, writing, and producing music in my band, Blue Rose, and later touring the country in the hit-making band, The Grass Roots.

There were many adventures on the road and I could fill a book just with those stories. Most of them were great fun but some were very serious. Remember, we were very young men and prone to do foolish things as young men will. In some cases we were treated like privileged characters and we tended to take full advantage of that.

On one tour, it was necessary that we fly on private airplanes because time constraints did not allow for us to fly commercial. So our management booked us on private planes allowing us to get in and out of cities very quickly. And it was nice. No waiting for luggage or walking through airports carrying bags or attaché cases or jackets or tape recorders. No, just walk off the plane to a waiting car and on to the concert or the hotel. Very nice indeed.

One of those nights after the show we went back to the hotel and some of us wound up in the bar. I was talking to the pilot and we were drinking and talking to a couple of girls when I thought it would be really great fun to take the girls up for a plane ride. After all, I knew the pilot and he had the keys. So we took off for the airport and he warmed up the plane.

I don't remember the city we were in but I do remember the four of us going up in the plane and flying over that city. The pilot turned the plane on its side so that the girl sitting in the co-pilot's seat could almost fall into his lap as we flew around. At one point he put the plane in a stall so that we could experience zero gravity, or weightlessness. Beer drifted up out of its bottle and seemed to hang in midair as we dived toward the earth floating momentarily above the seats. We landed shortly after that and we went back to the hotel and, I assume, to the bar. The next day I told Rob Grill, the leader of The Grass Roots, about the flight and he was furious. "Who's going to pay for the gas, and what about the insurance?" he yelled. I shrugged my shoulders and we left for the next city and the next show.

I am not proud of these irresponsible actions. I'm just sharing what it was like to be on the road with a rock band in those days and what some of us did in our craziness. There are more of these stories but much more of it would not really serve any useful purpose, if you get the picture. I am truly fortunate to be here relatively intact, mentally and physically. Now, take a look below and feast your eyes on '60s cool. Well, I thought it was at the time.

Me in the 1960s

Chapter Eight:
Dick Clark's American Bandstand
And
Caravan Of Stars Tour

During one of our Grass Roots tours, we performed on two of Dick Clark's shows. One, of course, was *American Bandstand* and the other was the Caravan of Stars tour. The shows that stand out the most in my mind were in Birmingham and Montgomery, Alabama. The performers on those shows were some of the biggest stars in show business. The Carpenters, Kenny Rogers and the First Edition, Neil Diamond, Iron Butterfly, and Blues Image. As for those of you I've left out, please forgive me but it has been forty years.

The shows were only twenty minutes long and we shared guitar amplifiers and PA systems to cut down on long breaks between acts. The sound systems of the time were not nearly as good as they are today. Wherever we played, we had to do the best we could with the sound systems that were supplied. As I mentioned earlier in this book, we were rarely able to hear ourselves, especially our voices.

We had rehearsed before these tours to be sure that we had our vocal parts as tight and as clean as we could get them, knowing full well that we probably wouldn't be able to hear them very well. This was not the case on the Caravan of Stars shows in Alabama.

Dick Clark

The Carpenters were a vocal band. They had a state-of-the-art PA system that allowed them to hear each other beautifully. All the acts used this system. We followed The Carpenters on one of the shows, and when we heard ourselves sing it startled us completely. We had never heard ourselves so well and it took us completely off guard. I remember that we looked at each other across the stage in complete amazement. We began listening

42

The Carpenters

so closely that we started to forget our parts. We cracked up laughing and a fun time was had by all.

Backstage at these shows was wonderful. We used to stand in the wings and watch the other acts while waiting our turn to go on.

The camaraderie and the jamming and the singing was as good as it gets. I can remember Kenny Rogers sitting at the piano in one of the dressing rooms playing and singing, and encouraging all of us to join in. I loved doing that. When I look back on it now I realize just how wonderful that was.

All of the guys in The Grass Roots lived in and around the Los Angeles area. It was home base. We recorded there, rehearsed there and had our photo shoots there. We also appeared on *American Bandstand* from time to time. I had been watching this show since I was a teenager. We always tuned into the show after school and were able to see all the top artists perform their latest hit records. Little did I know that one day I would be a guest on that show. And more than once.

Dick Clark always made us feel very much at home when we did the show. He was very friendly and always called us by our first names. He interviewed us very casually about what we were doing and our families and then we lip-synced our latest release. We were usually between tours and maybe in the recording studio when we did his show, so there was no pressure for us to get to the airport or the next show. It was all low key and great fun. You had to be there, and I was!

Chapter Nine:
Hanging Out
With Elvis In 1965

O ne of the greatest moments of my life was one I took for granted when it happened, but when I look back at it now I realize just how incredible it was. On a beautiful summer night back in 1965 I was invited to visit Elvis on the set of one of his movies. Larry Geller, my soon-to-be brother-in-law, was working for Elvis as his hairdresser and he invited me to the set to hang out with Elvis at the MGM Studios and watch him shoot his newest movie. It was a cool Southern California night, and I arrived as they were shutting down the day's shooting. Larry had told Elvis that I was an up-and-coming musician, and asked him if he wouldn't mind spending a few minutes with me to talk music and to encourage me about the business. Actually, I don't remember much about that part of the conversation at all but what I do remember was truly unbelievable.

Elvis was the most easy-to-be-around person you would ever want to know. He didn't have to work at it to make you comfortable around him, you just were. I did not find him to be egocentric or big-headed or anything like that. As a matter of fact I found him to be exactly the opposite. He was kind and personable and funny and he didn't take himself too seriously at all.

He asked me if I had ever sat behind one of the movie cameras that they used to film these movies. I told him I hadn't, and he told me to sit down in the seat of one of the camera operators. He then proceeded to instruct me on how to use the crank handles on the camera to follow the actors around. Then he acted out a scene where he picked up a rock from the ground and told me to use the cranks to follow him around. Elvis was acting out a scene for me.

After that we were walking toward the cars in the parking lot with Elvis in the lead when he just stopped and threw his hands in the air in one of his karate stances and said, "Hold it!" He then turned to a carnival set that had some balloons attached to a helium tank. He proceeded to take one of the balloons and suck the helium out of it.

Then he smiled and started singing "Love Me Tender" in the cartoon voice that the helium produces and everyone just fell out laughing, including Elvis. If there was ever a time when you had to be there this was it, and I was! How cool is that?

Chapter Ten:
Larry Geller
Early mentor

When I was sixteen years old I met a couple of girls on a street in my neighborhood. They went on to play a huge part in my life, and they are still in my life today. They were known as the Geller twins, Judy and Elaine. They were thirteen years old at the time and Elaine became my girlfriend. They had an older brother named Larry and his influence on my life was huge.

Larry Geller's Mom,
Annabelle Geller

When I was about eighteen, Larry turned me on to some books that would change my life. They

49

were books about spirituality. Why I was so interested in these things at such a young age I really don't know. I was raised in the Catholic religion and I really couldn't wait to get away from it. But the things Larry talked about really got my interest. I now know that his mother, Annabelle, was a guiding force in his knowledge and understanding of the spiritual life, and I was fortunate to have had him as a mentor. I was not the only one.

When Larry was working as a hairdresser for Jay Sebring (yes, the same one that was killed by the Manson family during the murders at the Sharon Tate/Roman Polanski house), he got a phone call to come to the home of Elvis Presley to cut his hair. It was at that meeting that he became Elvis' hairdresser and friend, and spiritual advisor. He remained in that position for many years and was with Elvis until he died. He even did his hair for the burial.

Chapter Eleven:
Albert King

Albert King was, in my opinion, the greatest electric blues guitar player that ever lived. He was my guitar hero. Nobody else before or after Albert played with such style, tone, phrasing, and feeling. His passion for the music and his passion for the guitar had very little to do with the right way to play it. He played left handed, guitar turned upside down, tuned to a minor chord, used his thumb for a pick, and used mostly down strokes and rarely played any rhythm. There were and are many great blues guitar players but, for me, Albert was the greatest because he created a style of playing that is so good, it has been copied by every other blues guitar player. Imagine trying to come up with a totally new style of playing right now. Where would you start? Albert just felt it.

He was a big man of over six feet tall, about 250 pounds, and he had very big hands. To watch him bend the strings to a high note and then stand on his tiptoes and dance was incredible. He felt every note and he shared it with us.

I first met Albert in 1968 at the Brass Ring, a nightclub in Sherman Oaks, California, where I was playing with my band, Blue Rose. My manager at the time, Gene Simmons (no relation to the Kiss member), was a good friend of Albert's manager, so he arranged for Albert to come and hear the band and for me to meet him. I was so excited to meet my guitar hero.

He was very gracious and very nice to me and to the band. As a matter of fact he liked the band so much that he asked us to tour with him and be his backup band. I was so blown away to think that he asked us to do this, and he said half-jokingly, "But there is only one lead guitar player on the stage. And it's me." Blue Rose had so much going on at this time that it was impractical to go on the road with Albert after all the work we had done with the band, but I was still honored to have been asked. He then invited me to go to lunch with him at the Original Pantry Cafe, a very well-known restaurant in downtown Los Angeles. I still have a big blown-up picture of us together standing in front of his bus hanging on the wall in my music room. I treasure it.

After that, from time to time, I would go to see him play when he was in town, and he would always get me backstage passes so that we could say "hi," and I would watch him play. He would bend his head down and look over his glasses to see if I was watching and then give me a smile, especially when he was happy with what he was playing and he knew that I knew it was really good.

Me and the 'guitar man' – Albert King

After one of the shows I went to his motel to hang out with him and his band and it was there that I picked up his guitar and realized how heavy the strings were and that it was tuned to a minor chord. That's what I remember anyway. Hanging out with Albert. How Cool!

The next time I saw Albert was in Memphis in 1974. I was touring with The Grass Roots and we had a layover in Memphis. I was going to the airport in the hotel shuttle when I saw Albert standing there as I got off the bus.

I had missed the first bus and so I was alone when I arrived at the terminal in the second one. Albert said, "Didn't I tell you never to be late. It ain't professional to be like that." He was playing around with me and then he invited me to breakfast. The other guys in the band couldn't believe that I was so friendly with Albert King. His influence on my playing can be heard on the solo in "Temptation Eyes," The Grass Roots' hit. I was given a gold record just for the solo on that record. I treasure the memories of my times with my guitar hero.

Thanks, Albert!

Chapter Twelve:
Iron Butterfly

In 1966, I was asked by Larry Geller, my former
brother-in-law and Elvis' hairdresser, to produce
and work with a band he found called Mother Goose.
They were from San Diego, California, and I eventually
moved there and joined the band. We were regulars at a
place called The Palace Bar, a typical sixties psychedelic
ballroom with light shows and projected bubble art and
very loud music.

It was there that I met and split sets with Iron
Butterfly. The band was a five-piece combo featuring
guitar, keyboards, bass, and drums and a totally amazing
dancer, named Darryl DeLoach. Doug Engle was the
keyboardist in this band and I believe he was the leader.
It was very unusual to have a dancer in a band but he was
mesmerizing to watch and the girls loved him. Eventually

Iron Butterfly – look at that hair!

we all moved to L.A. to get signed by a record company and record an album. They did. I remember them calling us to borrow amplifiers so that they could open at the Whisky A-Go-Go, which was the "in" spot of the time where all the big names of the day would play and promote their latest music. About this time, the band was staying in a house they rented in the Hollywood Hills. One night the boys went out on the town and left Doug, the keyboard player, at home and when they came back he was very drunk. They asked what he had been doing while they were gone, and he said he wrote a song. They asked, "What's it called," and he replied, "In-a-Gadda-Da-Vida." They wrote it down. The next day they asked him what "In-a-Gadda-da-Vida" meant and he said he didn't know. They said that he had told them that was the name of the song he had written. He said "No, No!" The name of the song I wrote was "In a Garden of Eden."

When they left on their first tour Doug borrowed a straw hat from me. He still owes me that hat.

Chapter Thirteen:
Phil Spector

When I grew up in Southern California there was a place called the Borscht Belt. It was a Jewish area of West Los Angeles near Fairfax and Melrose Avenue. I went to Fairfax High School, and I lived in what is now considered West Los Angeles.

When I was sixteen I met a set of twin girls that were to play a huge part in my life. They are the Geller girls, Judy and Elaine. We became very close then and are still very close now. As a matter of fact, I married Elaine but we divorced a short time later. Their brother Larry was to play a big part in my life and spiritual development. He turned me on to a wonderful new way of thinking that he received from his mother, Annabelle, and which he shared with me and Elvis, too, because he was Elvis' hairdresser for many years.

Larry was a schoolmate of a guy named Phil Spector. The way I first met Phil was through a friend who took me to Gold Star Recording Studios in Hollywood. It was there that I met Phil when he was producing records and writing songs that were to feature the legendary "Wall Of Sound" (also called the Spector Sound). We used to hang out at Gold Star and listen to what Phil was doing. When I say we, I am referring to Brian Wilson, the genius behind The Beach Boys, and Sonny Bono of Sonny & Cher. I was in good company sitting between the two of them on the floor outside the studio.

I have already mentioned the Borscht Belt and on Fairfax Avenue there was a pool hall called Mother's. I used to go to Mother's from time to time with the Geller twins' father, Bernie, and we would see Phil Spector there. He was always dressed in black with dark sunglasses and he always struck me as a little strange. He was with his bodyguard and he would just seem to watch people playing pool.

This was in 1965 and, although I didn't see Phil very much after that, I heard all about his eccentric ways and weird stories about guns in the studios, and his kidnapping John Lennon and his chauffeur-driven VW bus.

The last time I saw Phil was at Devonshire Sound

Studios in North Hollywood where I was working as a studio manager at night. I hadn't seen Phil in years but he remembered me, and we exchanged hellos

Phil Spector

and it was all very pleasant. He went to work and later in the night he got drunk on Manischewitz wine and proceeded to call Ronnie Spector, his wife at the time and singer of The Ronettes, and he started screaming at her on the phone. Part of my duties as manager of the studio was to check in with the clients at the start of my shift. When I checked in with Phil, he said, "What do you want, asshole?" We were old friends only the night before.

Fast forward to 2009 and Phil was convicted of second-degree murder and sentenced to nineteen years to life in prison for shooting and killing Lana Clarkson at his home in California. We all wondered why it took so long.

Chapter Fourteen:
Charles Manson

This story is one that always gives me the creeps. In 1968 I was involved in starting a new band with Joel Scott Hill on guitar, soon to be in The Flying Burrito Brothers, Nino Candido on guitar, son of Candy Candido, a famous movie comedian from the Forties, Bob Newkirk Jr. on drums, and bassist Chris Ethridge, also soon to be in The Flying Burrito Brothers.

We were rehearsing at Nino's house when a friend of his, Eric Jacobson, came to hear us perform. He said he liked what he heard and that he would like his friend Terry Melcher to hear what we were doing. Terry Melcher was the producer of The Byrds and Paul Revere & the Raiders

Charles Manson

at Columbia Records. He also was the son of Doris Day, the famous actress.

We were invited to Melcher's home to audition for him. He lived with Mark Lindsay, lead singer of Paul Revere & the Raiders, in the hills above the Beverly Hills area.

I remember the room and the wood beam in the ceiling.

We played some songs for Melcher and, as I remember, they were very rough and Melcher asked us to keep on working but we were not ready yet.

Around this time it is my understanding that Dennis Wilson of The Beach Boys introduced Charles Manson to Terry Melcher in the hopes that Melcher would produce him. Yeah, *that* Charles Manson. He auditioned and Terry passed on producing him.

Later that year, Terry Melcher sold that house to Roman Polanski and his wife, Sharon Tate. Manson didn't know that. So in seeking revenge for Terry Melcher turning him down he sent the Manson Family to kill him. What happened next can only be described as one of the most horrible murders in history. It is still eerie to think I was in that room.

A detective points to the beam in the Polanski house

Chapter Fifteen:
The Band at Momma's

In the early sixties I used to go to a place on Pico Boulevard in L.A. called Alvoturno's or "Momma's," as we called it back then. This was the first "club" I went to and my first exposure to the night life. Momma's daughter was Timi Yuro, who had a big hit record with "I'm So Hurt" at that time. The restaurant/bar was a favorite night spot where we used to go to hear live music and dance the night away. The list of musicians that played there is amazing. Where some of these guys would go and what they would go on to do is way beyond anything anyone could have possibly imagined!

The band that played at "Momma's" consisted of the following musicians:

Jim Gordon – Drums

I first met Jim in the early sixties when he was playing at "Momma's." Jim was sixteen at that time and was already playing with the Everly Brothers. My cousin Pat, Jim Gordon, and I used to go to the Pancake House after hours and talk the night away. A great guy to hang out with and talk about music and girls. Jim was to become one of the best and most successful drummers in the world. As a session drummer the list of hits and stars he played with is legendary.

The next time I saw Jim, he was playing with Delaney & Bonnie at the Brass Ring in Sherman Oaks. It was in this band that he hooked up with Eric Clapton, George Harrison and Ringo Starr, and eventually joined up with Delaney's bassist Carl Radle, and keyboard player Bobby Whitlock, to become Derek and the Dominoes with Eric Clapton, and writing "Layla" with Eric. Tragedy struck Jim when schizophrenia caused him to kill his mother in 1983. He died in prison at age 77 in March 2023.

Elliot Ingber – Lead Guitar

My guitar teacher and band member of the Fraternity of Man, and the co-writer of "Don't Bogart That Joint" from the film *Easy Rider*. Elliot also played with Frank Zappa and The Mothers of Invention and The Marketts. I will be eternally grateful to Elliot for the hours of instruction he selflessly gave me with never a thought of payment. I play the guitar because I love it, and I love Elliot for showing me how to do it.

Mike Post – aka Mike Postil – Keyboards

Mike's list of credits would fill a book. He is no doubt the most successful writer of TV and movie themes ever. Along with Pete Carpenter, he is responsible for *The A-Team*, *Hill Street Blues*, *Law and Order*, *NYPD Blue*, and *The Rockford Files*, just to name a few. He was musical director for *The Andy Williams Show,* and played guitar on Sonny and Cher's "I Got You Babe." He won five Grammys. He also played with Elliot Ingber (see above) and The Marketts. And, yes, he was the piano player in the band at Momma's.

Marshall Leib – Bass Player

Marshall was a member, along with Annette Kleinbard, aka Carol Conners, and Phil Spector, in the pop group The Teddy Bears, who had a big hit in 1958 with "To Know Him Is To Love Him." He also was a member of the group The Hollywood Argyles, whose hit was "Alley Oop." He produced Clydie King, who would one day pair up with Delaney and sing on one of my records. Marshall would let me borrow Gibson amplifiers that he used to store for the Everly Brothers when they didn't need them so that we had decent amps to rehearse with when we were starting out. We also used to box records up for him at his house on Gardner Street in Hollywood when he had his own record company, so that he could distribute them to different people. Marshall was a car guy and at that time drove a red Ferrari. In 2002 he was on his way to a car cruise night in Northridge, California, when he had a massive heart attack and died. He was the bass player in the Band at Momma's.

You had to be there, and I was!

Chapter Sixteen:
Earl Palmer

I have been fortunate to have been around since the beginning of rock and roll. My early memories of it would make me about ten years old, growing up on the streets of Manhattan, hearing doo-wop groups at Louie's candy store on 100th street and 1st Ave.

When I moved to California in 1954, the song I most remember is "Sh-boom." I first heard it in New York and then in California. But the biggest impact this music had on me came when I heard Little Richard, Fats Domino, and Huey "Piano" Smith and the groove music that I later learned was recorded in New Orleans. The common ingredient in this music was the drummer, Earl Palmer.

Now I didn't know that it was the beat in this music that made me love it so much, but after playing music for quite a while I came to realize that it had a lot to do with it. And it was Earl Palmer who was the drummer on most of those records.

Fast forward. In 1964 my first group, The Furlongs, which included my brother Kevin (drums), my cousin Patrick (lead guitar), Jeff Hittelman (bass), and me on guitar, hooked up with a record producer named Bob Field and made our first record.

During this association, Bob, who, along with Joe Saraceno, owned the group, The Marketts, an instrumental group which had a big hit with "Out of Limits," asked me if I had any instrumental songs I'd written. I said yes, and went home to write one. Always say "Yes" when opportunity knocks.

The next thing I knew we were at Western United recording studios in L.A., and I was in the studio with the best musicians in town about to record one of my songs. The James Bond secret agent fad was very popular at this time, so all the songs for this album had that theme. Mine was called "Napoleon's Solo", after a character on the TV show, *Man from Uncle*.

During the session it was decided that tambourine was needed on my song. So Joe asked me to play it. I had never played tambourine before, especially in the studio. And with the best musicians in town. I played it so hard that I soon had blisters all over my hands. I'm sure everyone had a good laugh. The drummer on the session told me to play easier, to watch him, and to hit the tambourine when his hand hit the snare drum. "Just watch me," he said.

Earl Palmer

Many years later I was playing with a band I had put together for a church I was attending in Eugene, Oregon, and the drummer in the band asked me about studio drummers I had worked with in L.A. He then asked me if I had worked with Earl Palmer.

I said, "Probably. What does he look like?"

He said, "He's a black cat, and he was one of the most in demand drummers in L.A."

I said "Oh yeah. He played on one of my songs The Marketts recorded."

"Wow" he said. "You played with Earl Palmer? The drummer that played on all the Little Richard and Fats Domino records?"

I said "WHAT?"

I didn't know until that moment that all those years ago on The Marketts session I had played with the man who had so influenced me when I was just a kid.

You had to be there, and I was!

73

Chapter Seventeen:
Don Everly

In 1979 I was playing in a nightclub called Sardo's in Burbank, California, in a trio consisting of Lynn Coulter on drums and vocals (he is now playing with Rita Coolidge), and Bill Armstrong on trumpet, keyboards, and vocals, who was recently playing with The Eagles.

One night, my old friend Joey Page came in to say hello, and happened to bring an old friend of his, Don Everly. Joey was at one time the bass player in the band that backed The Everly Brothers. He has, from time to time, shared vocals with Don or Phil when one or the other was not able to perform.

When I was just a kid The Everly Brothers were just about the biggest stars in rock 'n roll. Their harmonies were legendary. And still are! "Bye Bye Love," "Wake

Up Little Suzie," "All I Have To Do Is Dream," "Bird Dog," "Till I Kissed You," "When Will I Be Loved," and "Cathy's Clown" were among the biggest songs of the day.

On this particular night Don Everly and Joey were out on the town. They came by to have a drink, and I was thrilled to see them in the audience. On the next break I went over to say hello, and Joey suggested Don get up and sing with us. None of us were feeling any pain at this time, and it was suggested that we sing "Let It Be Me," one of The Everly Brothers hit songs. This song was not one of the songs that I knew all of the chord changes to, so I tried to "fake it."

Don Everly

To say it was disastrous would be an understatement. We finished the song, we had a good laugh and sat down. During this break I asked Bill, the keyboard player, if he was familiar with the song, and he said "No. I never heard it before." So I asked him if he knew who it was that he just played with. He said "No." I told him that he had just played with one of *The Everly Brothers*. He said, "Never heard of 'em." I told him who they were and that without them we wouldn't have the harmonies of The Beatles or Simon & Garfunkel or Crosby, Stills

& Nash. He was then very impressed by what had just taken place. He was a lot younger than Don, Joey, or me and had probably not heard The Everly Brothers on the radio like we had.

It wasn't long ago that I was reminiscing with a friend and I told this story. I then realized that I had actually <u>sang</u> with one of the true legends of rock 'n roll. I <u>sang</u> with one of the Everly Brothers. Not many can say that. You had to be there, and I was!

Chapter Eighteen:
Don Johnson And
Edward James Olmos

This story always brings a smile to my face because you just never know what can happen from a simple phone call from a friend returning a favor for you doing him a favor – especially when you didn't even expect it.

In another part of this book, I tell about a friend of mine, Chet McCracken, drummer and percussionist and former member of the Doobie Brothers. Chet used to play on all the demos that I worked on when I was a producer at Devonshire Studios.

One day I got a call from Chet asking if I wanted to play guitar on a recording session he was doing with Don Randi, a fine session pianist and the owner of The Baked Potato, a jazz nightclub in North Hollywood. During the session I noticed that there were a couple of guys looking through the glass window of the control room and pointing at me. I figured I was not playing what they wanted to hear. Then Chet said that they were the producers of the movie that this session was for and they wanted to know if I would be interested in being an extra in the movie. It seems that they were having a difficult time with one of the background actors and wanted to replace him and that I looked a lot like him.

The movie was called *Undercover Angels* (I think that was the title, although I can't find it listed as that or anything else from 1974 through 1979) and it starred Don Johnson who at that time was not the big star he was to become. As a matter of fact, I didn't even know who he was. He played the part of a singing secret agent and we played his band, also secret agents. The movie also starred Vince Edwards of the *Dr. Ben Casey* TV series fame, and George Lazenby who played James Bond in *Her Majesty's Secret Service* in 1969. Don and I became working buddies, and we shared a common interest in music and in playing the guitar.

What does this have to do with Edward James Olmos? Well as you may know Don Johnson and Edward James Olmos eventually joined up in the TV series *Miami Vice* but I always knew him as Eddie James. He was a good friend of mine and Delaney Bramlett's, and he lived across the street from Delaney. He was a singer and dancer in a band that I eventually produced for United Artists called Elijah. I used to see him at wrap parties for different studios and at recording sessions around town, and I always liked him a lot. I never knew he would be such a big star but whoever knows. I remember seeing him on billboards around town promoting *Zoot Suit* in which he had the lead role, El Pachuco.

Isn't it just amazing how this stuff works and the synchronicity of it all? You had to be there, and I was!

Chapter Nineteen:
From Blue Rose
to The Doobie Brothers

I had to call drummer Chet McCracken to make sure I remembered this story factually and, as it turned out, I pretty much had it right. Who would have thought that three guys that were in my band at different times would wind up in the Grammy Award-winning group, The Doobie Brothers. But it happened!

Michael McDonald, Willie Weeks, and Chet McCracken were all in my band, Blue Rose, before they were in The Doobie Brothers. I was very fortunate to have shared the stage with such talented musicians. As I look back, it is something I remember with great pride. To quote Delaney Bramlett, "These guys could pick!"

The first guys to join Blue Rose were Willie Weeks, bass player, and Bill Lordan, drummer. Bill Lordan would go on to play with Robin Trower of Procol Harum fame. They were from Minneapolis, and I first met them through members of a band called Gypsy that I was sharing a house with in the now famous Laurel Canyon in the Hollywood Hills. I had a few gigs around town and I needed a bass player and drummer to complete Blue Rose. So, they came out and we started rehearsing, and they moved into the Laurel Canyon house.

Willie was really dedicated to his bass playing, and I remember him getting up and first thing lighting up a Newport cigarette and starting to practice. He had a turntable right next to his bed. He learned to play everything he could get his hands on. He was a great player even then. Today he plays bass with Eric Clapton, after playing and recording with some of the best artists there are, including Wynonna Judd and Vince Gill. His bass solo on Donny Hathaway's *Live* album is a classic performance and a must-hear for every bass player. And he was in my band.

When we finished The Blue Rose album and made our record deal with Clive Davis, he put us on Epic Records, a subsidiary of Columbia Records. I needed a touring band and I especially needed a singer with a high voice who played keyboards. Someone gave me Michael

McDonald's number. I called him and we got together. At the time I really didn't realize just how great he was. He sang with a little Ray Charles influence and he played that way too. I was singing most of the songs, so I needed someone to sing high harmony and play piano. I remember asking him if he would sing a couple of songs during the show so that I could rest my voice.

He said he would, and I asked him to sing some of his original songs so that I could see if I thought they would fit in the set. I didn't like them very much so I passed on them. I passed on Michael McDonald's songs that probably included "Takin' it to the Streets" and "It Keeps You Running." I can't believe I did that, but I did!

I have seen Michael several times since then, and we always share a good laugh about those days.

Me and Michael McDonald

85

When Michael joined the band we were playing in a nightclub in the San Fernando Valley, California, and some of the younger musicians used to sneak in to hear us play. One of these guys was Jeff Porcaro, a drummer who would become one of the best and most highly regarded drummers in the world. Along with his brothers they became Toto, and at one time Jeff was touring with Steely Dan. He contacted Michael, and Michael began playing with Steely Dan also. When The Doobie Brothers' singer couldn't make a tour, Michael was asked to go and then was invited to join the band. The rest is history. Michael is one of the greatest singers and songwriters I have ever known. I gave him one of his first gigs in L.A., and he sang harmony in my band. Wow!

Chet McCracken and I met up in the San Fernando Valley probably in the early seventies. I was producing music for Devonshire Studios Productions about this time and playing some local venues, and Chet and I hooked up. He then began playing drums on all the demos that I produced at Devonshire. I'd like to think that I had something to do with his success in the studio but that would be silly. He had lots of talent and was very hard working in the pursuit of his craft. His list of credits includes Stevie Nicks, Rita Coolidge, Hank Williams Junior, Joe Walsh, Michael McDonald and The Doobie Brothers, just to name a few.

Chet now lives in the San Fernando Valley, and has his own recording studio where he engineers and produces music for a variety of artists and musicians, as well as writing and creating his own music.

Chapter Twenty:
John Hammond Jr.

I just had to look at a CD I recently ordered from the Internet to see when it was recorded. It said 1971/72 on the CD. That seems about right and means I worked with Delaney more than I remembered. I don't remember how it came about, but he asked me to play on an album he was producing for John Hammond Jr. At the time I was not all that familiar with John's work, but I was happy to be recording another project with Delaney. What an honor that turned out to be!

John Hammond's father was a record producer for Columbia Records, and he was responsible for producing or discovering some of the biggest talents the music business has ever known. This list includes Billie Holiday, Benny Goodman, Aretha Franklin, Bob Dylan,

John Hammond Jr.

Bruce Springsteen, and Stevie Ray Vaughan, to name just a few. He also was responsible for reissuing Robert Johnson's music, the undisputed "King of the Delta Blues Singers," who was a big influence on John Jr.

Back to the session.

The album took about a week or so to record, and Delaney and John were writing at night and we were recording at Sunset Sound studios during the day. At one point we had finished all the songs that they had prepared, and they had finally run out of songs. Delaney pushed the talkback button and asked if anyone had any songs that would be good for John. By this time I realized just what an incredible talent John was. He was a real blues man. He played guitar and harmonica, and sang in the style of the Black blues men of the Mississippi Delta. I was a little hesitant to say anything but none of the other guys on the session did, so I bit the bullet and got up the nerve and said, right then and there, "I might have a song." He didn't say,

"Send me a demo later" or "Show it to me after the session," he said "OK, play it for us now!" So, I played a song I had written called "Man In The Road." It was a blues influenced three-chord song with a syncopated groove that I thought would be good for John. They liked it and Delaney told me to teach it to the band, and we recorded it right then. I was recently given a vinyl copy of the original record as a gift. The definition of luck is: "When preparation meets opportunity."

You had to be there, and I was!

Chapter Twenty-One:
Ray Charles

When I was working at Britannia Studios, Tom Jones's studio in North Hollywood, I had the opportunity to work with some truly legendary people in the entertainment business.

At one time Clint Eastwood was making some movies that featured guest artists that were not necessarily actors but more singers and stars in the music business. *Any Which Way You Can* was one of those films. It was in these films that he performed duets with major singing stars and Ray Charles was one of them. "Beers To You" is a song they recorded for the movie *Any Which Way You Can*.

The day that "Beers to You" was recorded Clint was very nervous because he, a truly fine actor, was about to record with the legendary Ray Charles, one of the greatest singers that ever was.

As a young boy I was always listening to the radio, as were all of my friends. Ray Charles' record of "What'd I Say" was a favorite of all the listeners and was played by all the bands at the time. He went on to have many hits and he was a legend even then. I have seen him perform live and listening to him sing was as good as it gets.

Ray Charles

When he arrived that day on the arm of his valet, we had him set up in the hallway because the main studio was completely full of equipment ready for the next session, which, as I remember, was for the soundtrack for a movie.

I had set up a microphone and speakers since Ray didn't use headphones that day. I also set up a music stand for him. Ray positioned himself in front of the mic and then placed his music, which was in Braille, on the stand. He asked for a cup of water and asked the engineer to roll tape and he sang it in a couple of takes. It was incredible to be standing within feet of that voice. He then graciously thanked everyone and left on the arm of his valet. The consummate pro. Never did it occur to me that one day I would be in the studio working with Ray Charles.

You had to be there, and I was!

Chapter Twenty-Two:
David Foster

In 1992, I was working at Devonshire Studios, another recording facility in North Hollywood, as a night studio manager. David Foster, writer and producer of the group Chicago and many others – his resume could make his own book – was working on a Paul Simon song, "Still Crazy After All These Years," for Ray Charles, and "I will Always Love You" for Whitney Houston. I still have a rough cassette copy of Ray's version of the Paul Simon song.

It was one of those evenings that David was working under the most difficult set of circumstances. In the wee hours of the night before, he was driving home along Pacific Coast Highway when he accidentally – and literally – ran into Ben Vereen.

Ben is an internationally renowned actor best known for his role as Chicken George in the smash hit TV series, *Roots*. Ben is also an accomplished singer, dancer, and Broadway star. He was walking down an unlit stretch of Pacific Coast

Ben Vereen

Highway in a daze when he was struck by David Foster's car and almost killed. He was thrown about ninety feet, and it is a miracle that he survived.

David was devastated as he tried to work that night, and I saw him several times in the lounge holding his head in his hands trying to get over what had happened. Although the accident was not his fault, he was clearly traumatized by it. Who wouldn't be?

David Foster

Chapter Twenty-Three:
Cheech Marin

I was recording at Devonshire Studios in 1981 and so I was Cheech Marin.

I had a new guitar to show off, and I was excited to show it to my friends. The guitar was specially built for me by my cousin, Patrick. My cousin and I have the very unusual relationship of being double first cousins. His mother and my mother were sisters and his father and my father were brothers. We have always been very close, more like brothers than cousins. We are only six months apart in age and we share a fondness for the guitar, both in playing them and, in his case, building them.

This particular guitar was made of Hawaiian Koa, a very pretty, dense, and therefore, a very heavy wood. It was adorned with gold hardware and the inlay was absolutely beautiful. It had a blue rose, in recognition of my band of the same name, on the headstock, made of abalone and turquoise and the inlay was breathtaking.

Back to Cheech.

I was in the office of the studio and had just taken the guitar out of the case to show it to everyone when Cheech, who was on the phone, came over to us and wanted to get a look at what everyone was so curious to see. This is the funny part. He said, "Let me see that," and he reached his hands out to hold it. I gave it to him and he headed down the hallway saying, in the Chicano accent that he was so famous for," Oh, man, thank you *so* much! I don't know what to say." He was taking off with the guitar like I had given it to him as a gift and I had to yell at him, "Hey! Bring that back here!" He did and we all had a great laugh and went back to work. He was so quick and funny. You had to be there, and I was!

Cheech Marin

100

Chapter Twenty-Four:
Johnny Paycheck

I first saw Johnny Paycheck at the Grammy Awards in 1979 when he was nominated for Best Country and Western Vocal Performance. His song "Take This Job And Shove It," written by David Alan Coe, was nominated for Best Country and Western Song. I saw Johnny in the halls of the host hotel and he had on the biggest cowboy hat I had ever seen. He was so high he was bouncing off the walls. I am not telling tales out of school here, Johnny's problems with drugs and alcohol are well documented. That was the first time I saw him.

The next time I met up with him was in 1981. I was working as the night manager and second engineer at Britannia Studios in North Hollywood, which was owned by Tom Jones and his manager, Gordon Mills.

Johnny was there to record a tribute album of Merle Haggard songs to be produced by Merle Haggard himself. I had worked with Merle and his band before, and they were among nicest bunch of guys I've ever worked with. Merle's band was to back Johnny. The resulting album, *Mr. Hag Told My Story,* was recorded and my friendship with Johnny was formed. I would go to a couple of country nightclubs in the San Fernando Valley, and meet up with him and his road manager, Mike Maury, "The Kid." The owners of these places would keep them open until well after closing time so that Johnny and his friends could party all night. And we did.

It was at about this time that I wrote a song that just seemed to fit Johnny called "Bad Luck." It was kind of how his life was going at the time. He told me that he played the demo in the tour bus all the time and that he

Me and Johhny Paycheck

was eventually: "Gonna cut it." But it was not to be. Johnny seemed to have a lot of trouble with the law and eventually went to prison for shooting a guy in a bar fight. The song's lyrics go like this.

> Bad luck, bad luck, that's all I've ever known,
> I been down so long, up is all I can go.
> I'm always fallin' on bad times,
> Seems like I can't catch a roll.
> I'm always payin' for something I
> did, When I was out of control.
>
> But lately I'm keeping my nose clean,
> And I don't drink like I once did.
> But it doesn't matter whatever I do,
> Everything I touch just turns to…
>
> Bad luck, bad luck, that's all I've ever known,
> I been down so long up is all I can go.
>
> I'm always running on empty,
> I can't get outa the red.
> I always borrow to pay back tomorrow,
> At some godawful percent.
> But I dared to think things were changing,
> Somehow I got me a raise.
> But there must be a racket,
> Cause I jumped a bracket. Everything I
> touch just turns to…

Bad luck, bad luck, trouble's all I ever know,

I been down so long up is all I can go.

I never hung out with Johnny after that, but I'll never forget recording with a real "Outlaw." Johnny was the real thing – one of the best country singers that ever lived. I even hung out with David Alan Coe, the writer of Johnny's hit, "Take This Job And Shove It," at those sessions.

You had to be there, and I was!

Chapter Twenty-Five:
Good Sam and
the Old Guitar

In 2006 I went to visit my mom in the assisted care facility where she lived. As I was driving down the street I saw a woman collapsed in the street by the curb with a bicycle lying next to her. She had fallen and was obviously badly shaken up. I stopped to see if I could lend a hand and I asked her if I should call 9-1-1, or if she needed an ambulance. She said she didn't need one and I could see she was shaken but there didn't seem to be anything broken. She was just dirty and she did have road rash on her hands and some slight bleeding on her nose. She looked to be in her mid to late fifties and more dazed from the fall than anything else. I asked her if she wanted me to take her to the emergency room and she said, "No." I then asked her if she wanted me to take her home and she said, "Yes." She was still obviously shaken up.

So I dusted her off and helped her into my SUV. I then realized her bike needed to be put into the back of my car. I had given a guitar lesson earlier in the day so I had my old Yamaha acoustic guitar in the back seat without the case. The back seat was in the upright position so

I put the guitar on the sidewalk and proceeded to fold down the seat when I realized that I had my bike rack on the back of my vehicle. So I put her bike on the rack and got in to drive her home. It was a couple of miles drive to her house and when we arrived I helped her into the house. She then introduced me to a man named Bill; she was his caregiver. It was then when I went to take the bike off the rack that I realized that I had left my guitar on the sidewalk. I rushed back to get it and when I got back to the spot where I left it, it was gone.

I had owned this guitar for over forty years and I have written many, many songs on it including songs written when my son was born and other milestones in my life. It has been all over the country with me and if it could talk what a story it would tell. A great comfort in difficult times and great fun at parties and gatherings with friends. It was not worth a great deal of money but to me it was irreplaceable.

I called the police department and called the lost and found at the newspaper when I got home all the time trying to understand what lesson God had for me to learn. After all I was just trying to be a Good Samaritan and do the right thing and losing my guitar wasn't in my plan. That was Tuesday night.

The next day was a busy day filled with must do's

and there was no time to put up flyers and so I had to wait until Thursday to do it. I made up flyers that morning and went back to the spot where I lost the guitar and I saw a man painting the fence there and I told him about the lost guitar and asked him if he had seen it. He said he hadn't, so I looked around and noticed a row of apartments with a pathway with tall wooden fences in front of the apartments. They were all closed except for one.

It was about a fifty yards walk to the open wooden fence and there were a few kids' toys in the yard. The door to the apartment was open so I said, "Hello, anybody home?" A woman came to the door. I stood there with my flyers and told her about the lost guitar and she listened very quietly. After a little pause, she smiled and said, "I have the guitar." I was dumbfounded!

She then told the story of how her little girls, a five and a nine-year-old, had found the guitar on the sidewalk and thought somebody had thrown it away. The woman then told me the kids were playing with it and had broken a string on it and painted flowers and trees on it but she had it. She then went into the back of the apartment and brought it out.

I was dumbfounded. What are the chances? The first place I went, other than the man painting the fence, and I found it. I was completely astonished. She told me that her daughter wanted to learn how to play the guitar and I told her I would teach her, free of charge, as long as she wanted to take lessons.

I also told her that if she wanted to bring the kids to where I was playing, I play music at different places around Prescott, Arizona, that she could have anything on the menu she and the kids wanted. She did come, and she and the kids had dinner and that Saturday her nine-year-old had her first lesson. What's the lesson here? I'm sure there are many. Remember when I first lost the guitar I asked God why? I was just trying to help somebody and this is the thanks I get.

I learned gratitude for the little things in life. It was not an expensive guitar but it meant so much to me. Again, I learned to trust God and that He always has my best interests in mind even though I don't see it at the time.

I received a call from a woman that works in an office that I do business with from time to time to tell me that her father is the man that the woman who fell takes care of, and that she was all right and she thanked me for being the Good Samaritan. Good Sam and the old guitar!

In Closing ...

As I was writing these stories down, I had the opportunity to relive those magical moments and it helped me realize just how much fun this was for me – and I hope, in the retelling, for you too. I'm fortunate not only to have lived them but to be able to share them with you now. If we should meet somewhere, sometime, come up and say hello. Please check out my website at www.terry-furlong.com.

Terry

www.ingramcontent.com/pod-product-compliance
Lightning Source LLC
Chambersburg PA
CBHW071326130626